FOSSILS

By Chris and Helen Pellant

Gareth Stevens
Publishing

Please visit our web site at **www.garethstevens.com**. For a free catalog describing Gareth Stevens Publishing's list of high-quality books, call 1-800-542-2595 (USA) or 1-800-387-3178 (Canada). Gareth Stevens Publishing's fax: 1-877-542-2596

Library of Congress Cataloging-in-Publication Data

Pellant, Chris.
    Fossils / Chris and Helen Pellant. — U.S. ed.
       p. cm. — (Rock stars)
    Includes index.
    ISBN-10: 0-8368-9223-2   ISBN-13: 978-0-8368-9223-9 (lib. bdg.)
    1. Fossils—Juvenile literature. I. Pellant, Helen. II. Title.
QE432.2.P449   2009
560—dc22   2008016116

This North American edition first published in 2009 by
Gareth Stevens Publishing
A Weekly Reader® Company
1 Reader's Digest Road
Pleasantville, NY 10570-7000 USA

This U.S. edition copyright © 2009 by Gareth Stevens, Inc. Original edition copyright © 2008 by ticktock Media Ltd. First published in Great Britain in 2008 by ticktock Media Ltd., 2 Orchard Business Centre, North Farm Road, Tunbridge Wells, Kent, TN2 3XF.

For ticktock:
Project Editor: Julia Adams   Project Designer: Emma Randall
Picture Researcher: Lizzie Knowles   With thanks to Graham Rich

For Gareth Stevens:
Senior Managing Editor: Lisa M. Herrington   Creative Director: Lisa Donovan
Senior Editor: Barbara Bakowski   Electronic Production Manager: Paul Bodley

Picture credits (t = top; b = bottom; c = center; l = left; r = right):
age fotostock/SuperStock: 20cr. Phil Degginger/Carnegie Museum/Alamy: 22ft. GeoScience: 19cl, 20tr. Herris.fr/SuperStock: 14–15t. iStock: 3E, K, 4bl, 4br, 12tl, 15b, 10cr, 24t. Jupiter Images: 21cr. M P Land/Science Photo Library: 16cr, 17tl. Greg Martin: SuperStock: 14bl. Astrid & Hanns-Frieder Michler/Science Photo Library: 19tl. Chris and Helen Pellant: 8bl, 10cl, 11tr, 13tr, 16tl, 16cl, 16bl, 16br, 17cl, 17bl, 18tl, 18cl, 18cr, 18bl, 18br, 19bl, 20bl, 20br, 21cl, 21bl, 23cl. Louie Psihoyos/Getty Images: 23cr. Graham Rich: 6. Mark A. Schneider/Science Photo Library: 16tr. Peter Scoones/Getty Images: 22c. Shutterstock: 1, 2, 3A, B, C, D, F, G, H, I, J, 4tl, 5t, 5b x3, 6tl, 8tl, 8–9c, 9t, 9b,10tl, 10–11 main, 11cr, 11br, 12, 13tl, 13bl, 13br, 14tl, 14br, 17r x4, 18tr, 19tr, 19br, 21tl, 21tr, 21br, 22t, 22b, 23tl, 23tr, 23bl, 23br. TH Foto-Werbung/Science Photo Library: 20cl. ticktock Media Archive: 7 all. Javier Trueba/MSF/Science Photo Library: 20tl.

Printed in the United States of America

2 3 4 5 6 7 8 9 10 09 08

Contents

Fossil Collector

Words that appear in **bold** are explained in the glossary.

What Are Fossils?

Earth formed more than 4 billion years ago. Plants and animals have lived on our planet for millions of years. **Fossils** are traces or remains of plants and animals that lived long ago. Fossils can be found in rock.

Many different animals can turn into fossils. Fossils tell us about life on Earth millions of years ago. Plant fossils help us understand what the **climate** and land were like then.

Fossils can form from tiny sea creatures.

Some fossils are of huge dinosaurs!

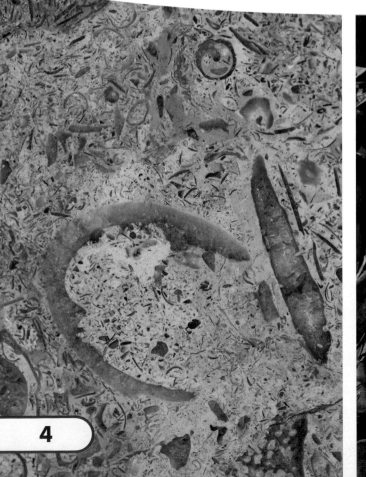

Fish fossils

Sometimes, we can compare fossils with living animals and plants. We can see how living things changed over millions of years. Many **fossilized** animals and plants have living relatives.

Fossils can also show which animals and plants changed little over time. The ginkgo tree, corals, and ferns look similar to the way they looked about 20 million years ago!

Ginkgo tree

Coral

Ferns

How Do Fossils Form?

Some fossils are the remains of dead animals and plants. They change and harden over millions of years.

Most animal fossils form in the same way.

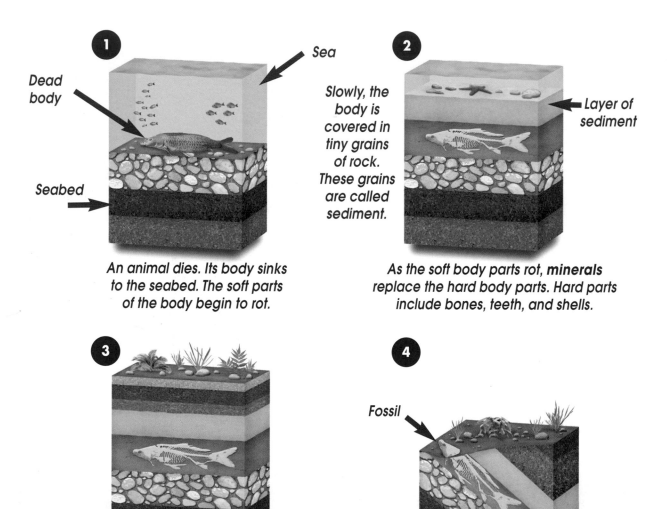

1

Sea

Dead body

Seabed

An animal dies. Its body sinks to the seabed. The soft parts of the body begin to rot.

2

Slowly, the body is covered in tiny grains of rock. These grains are called sediment.

Layer of sediment

As the soft body parts rot, **minerals** replace the hard body parts. Hard parts include bones, teeth, and shells.

3

The layers of sediment build up. The weight of the new layers squeezes the sediment below. **Sedimentary rock** forms around the body.

4

Fossil

Movements in Earth's surface sometimes shift the layers upward. Wind and rain wear down the rock around the fossil.

Time Line

We use a time line to show different times in Earth's history. It is broken up into **eras** and **periods**. You can see how much life on Earth has changed since plants and animals first appeared!

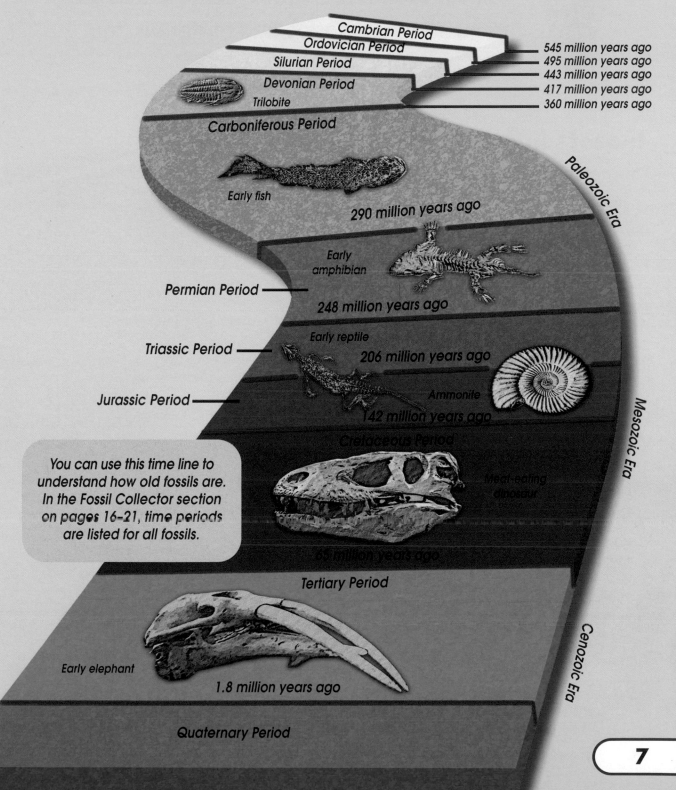

Cambrian Period — 545 million years ago
Ordovician Period — 495 million years ago
Silurian Period — 443 million years ago
Devonian Period — 417 million years ago
Trilobite — 360 million years ago

Carboniferous Period

Paleozoic Era

Early fish

290 million years ago

Early amphibian

Permian Period

248 million years ago

Early reptile

Triassic Period

206 million years ago

Jurassic Period

Ammonite

142 million years ago

Cretaceous Period

Mesozoic Era

Meat-eating dinosaur

You can use this time line to understand how old fossils are. In the Fossil Collector section on pages 16–21, time periods are listed for all fossils.

65 million years ago

Tertiary Period

Cenozoic Era

Early elephant

1.8 million years ago

Quaternary Period

Types of Fossils

Fossils can form in many ways. Most fossils form in sedimentary rock. Some fossils are found in other places and materials, too.

Insects in Amber >>

Sometimes small insects get trapped in the sticky **resin** of pine trees. The resin seals in the insects completely. Over time, the resin hardens and turns into **amber**. The insects are saved within the amber.

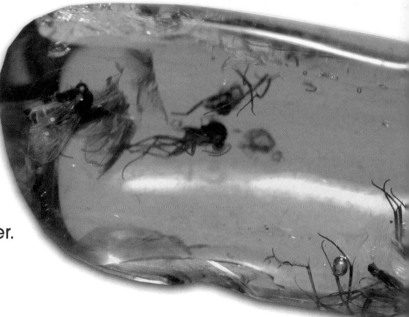

<< Shell Crystals

Ammonites were shelled animals that lived in the ocean long ago. The shells of ammonites are common as fossils in rock. The shells are divided into small parts called chambers. **Crystals** sometimes form in the chambers.

Dinosaur Footprint >>

If you walk on wet sand at the beach, you leave a trail of footprints. When dinosaurs wandered across a muddy riverbank, they left footprints, too.

As the mud dried out, layers of sediment washed into the tracks. The layers hardened, and the footprints became fossils.

Fossilized Wood >>

This piece of fossilized wood looks exactly as it did millions of years ago. As the wood rotted, hard minerals replaced every bit of it.

This fossilized wood is millions of years old.

Ocean Fossils

Earth has changed a lot over millions of years. Places that are now dry land were once covered by oceans. Large areas of the United States used to be underwater! People sometimes find fossils of ocean animals on land. Scientists have uncovered fossils of shark teeth and whale bones.

Giant Shark Tooth

Because a tooth is hard, it may be the only part of an animal that is fossilized. This tooth is about 3 inches (7.5 centimeters) long. It is from a giant shark called *Carcharodon*. *Carcharodon* lived during the Cenozoic Era. This shark grew to be more than 40 feet (12 meters) long. It was twice the size of today's great white shark!

Brittle Stars

Brittle stars looked like sea stars. Many of them crowded together on the ocean floor. Each brittle star had five long, thin arms with a small body in the center. These fossils came from Jurassic rocks. **Crinoid** fossils have been found in Jurassic rocks, too.

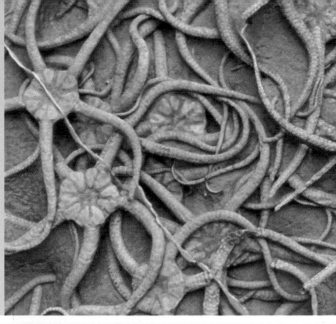

Trilobite

The trilobite was a small crab-like animal that lived on the seabed. Its hard outer shell was made of joined pieces. This trilobite had eyes on the ends of long stalks. It could see even when it was buried in the mud on the seafloor. This fossil is from the Ordovician Period.

Ammonite

The ammonite was a squid-like animal. It lived in the large, open end of its shell. Its **tentacles** hung out of the shell. This ammonite fossil is from the Jurassic Period. Some other shelled fossils are **brachiopods** (BRAY-kee-uh-pahdz) and **bivalves**.

Land Fossils

Fossils can tell us a lot about what Earth used to look like. Fossilized plants can tell us about the landscape. Fossils of animals can show where and how they lived and changed.

Bird (Archaeopteryx)

Archaeopteryx (ahr-kee-AHP-tuh-riks) looked like a small dinosaur with feathers. It was about the size of a pigeon. It probably glided. All *Archaeopteryx* fossils are from the Jurassic Period. We know that is when birds began to develop.

Mayfly

This fossilized mayfly was found in rocks from the Cretaceous Period. Mayflies become fossils only when very fine-grained mud covers them soon after they die. We know that this mayfly lived in a muddy area.

Fern

Fossils of fern-like plants from the Carboniferous Period look like ferns that grow today. This helps us understand what some landscapes might have looked like millions of years ago.

Albertosaurus Skull

Albertosaurus was a meat-eating dinosaur. It lived in the Cretaceous Period. Most *Albertosaurus* fossils were found very close together. Experts think these dinosaurs lived in big groups.

Amazing Fossil Places

Some places on Earth have amazing fossil finds. Sometimes the fossils are part of the landscape. You don't even have to hunt for them!

It's a Fact!

In the Petrified Forest, jewel-like crystals formed in cracks in the wood. They are a rainbow of sparkling colors!

Dinosaur Quarry, Utah

This area has more Jurassic dinosaur fossils than any other place in the world. People have found about 12,000 dinosaur bones here!

Petrified Forest, Arizona

Tree fossils are scattered across this huge area in Arizona. The fossils formed when the trees' rotting parts were slowly replaced by minerals. These fossils are made of a mineral called quartz.

Chalk Cliffs, Great Britain

Chalk is a soft, powdery rock. It is made up of millions of tiny pieces of fossil shells. These cliffs formed about 65 million years ago.

Coal Mines

Most rocks contain minerals, but coal does not. It is a sedimentary rock that formed from fossilized plants. Coal is dug from the ground in **mines**.

Fossil Collector

Brachiopod (Productus)

PERIOD: Ordovician to Permian
FOUND: worldwide
SIZE: 1.6 inches (4 cm)

Coral (Halysites)

PERIOD: Ordovician and Silurian
FOUND: worldwide
SIZE: groups 4 inches (10 cm) across

Graptolite (Didymograptus)

PERIOD: Ordovician
FOUND: worldwide
SIZE: 1 inch (2.5 cm)

Seed fern (Eupecopteris)

PERIOD: Carboniferous
FOUND: in the United States, Europe, and Asia
SIZE: 2 inches (5 cm)

Trilobite (Paradoxides)

PERIOD: Cambrian
FOUND: in Europe, North and South America, and northern Africa
SIZE: up to 24 inches (60 cm)

Trilobite (Phacops)

PERIOD: Silurian and Devonian
FOUND: in the United States, Europe, and northern Africa
SIZE: up to 6 inches (15 cm)

Coral
(Ketophyllum)

PERIOD: Silurian
FOUND: in Europe
SIZE: 3.2 inches (8 cm)

Trilobite
(Olenellus)

PERIOD: Cambrian
FOUND: in North America, Greenland, and
northwestern Scotland
SIZE: 3.2 inches (8 cm)

Trilobite
(Trimerus)

PERIOD: Silurian
FOUND: worldwide
SIZE: 8 inches (20 cm)

Getting Started

Before you go to look for fossils, you'll need to get some basic tools.

- a backpack for your tools and the fossils you find

- a rock hammer for breaking up loose rocks

- a chisel for splitting rock layers

- goggles to protect your eyes when hammering and chiseling

- a magnifying glass to see close-up details

- a notebook and a pencil to write details about fossils you find

- air-filled packing wrap and bags to protect and carry your fossils

Fossil Collector

Ammonite (Dactylioceras)

PERIOD: Jurassic
FOUND: worldwide
SIZE: 4 inches (10 cm)

Ammonite (Douvilleiceras)

PERIOD: Cretaceous
FOUND: in the United States, South America, Europe, and India
SIZE: 2 inches (5 cm)

Ammonite (Scaphites)

PERIOD: Cretaceous
FOUND: in the United States, southern Africa, Australia, and Chile
SIZE: 3 inches (7.5 cm)

Brachiopod (Terebratula)

PERIOD: Jurassic
FOUND: worldwide
SIZE: 1.2 inches (3 cm)

Crinoid (Pentacrinites)

PERIOD: Triassic to recent
FOUND: in the United States and Europe
SIZE: 3.3 feet (1 m)

Maidenhair tree (Ginkgo)

PERIOD: Permian to recent
FOUND: worldwide
SIZE: 1 inch (2.5 cm); tree 100 feet (30 m)

Ammonite (Perisphinctes)

PERIOD: Jurassic
FOUND: in Europe, Africa, and Japan
SIZE: 8 inches (20 cm)

Coral (Isastrea)

PERIOD: Jurassic and Cretaceous
FOUND: in the United States, Africa, and Europe
SIZE: 4 inches (10 cm)

Reptile (Ichthyosaurus)

PERIOD: Triassic, Jurassic, and Cretaceous
FOUND: worldwide
SIZE: 10 feet (3 m)

Finding Fossils

You may find fossils between the layers of sedimentary rock. Try to split the rock into flat slabs.

CAUTION: When splitting rocks, always ask an adult to help!

- Use a guidebook and a local map.

- **Limestone** and **clay** may have good fossils.

- Break up only loose rocks. Do not hammer cliffs or rock faces. Be sure to wear goggles for safety.

- Use a camera to take pictures of fossils that are too big to carry.

Fossil Collector

Bear tooth (Ursus)

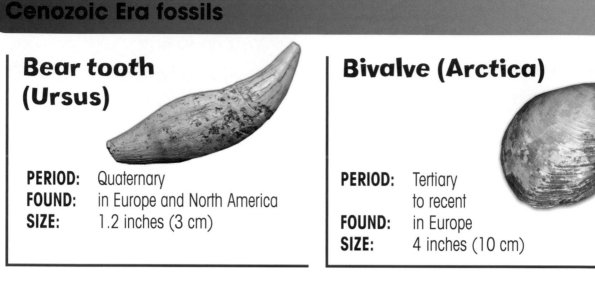

PERIOD: Quaternary
FOUND: in Europe and North America
SIZE: 1.2 inches (3 cm)

Bivalve (Arctica)

PERIOD: Tertiary
to recent
FOUND: in Europe
SIZE: 4 inches (10 cm)

Fish (Knightia)

PERIOD: Tertiary
FOUND: in the United States
SIZE: 10 inches (25 cm)

Maple leaf (Acer)

PERIOD: Tertiary to
recent
FOUND: worldwide
SIZE: 2 inches (5 cm)

Shark tooth (Lamna)

PERIOD: Cretaceous to recent
FOUND: worldwide
SIZE: 1.6 inches (4 cm)

Sponge (Siphonia)

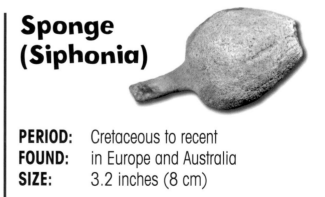

PERIOD: Cretaceous to recent
FOUND: in Europe and Australia
SIZE: 3.2 inches (8 cm)

Crab (Liocarcinus)

PERIOD: recent
FOUND: in Europe
SIZE: 5 inches (12.5 cm)

Sea urchin (Lovenia)

PERIOD: Tertiary to recent
FOUND: in Australia
SIZE: 2 inches (5 cm)

Tusk shells (Dentalium)

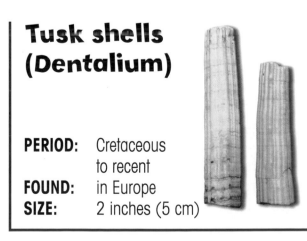

PERIOD: Cretaceous to recent
FOUND: in Europe
SIZE: 2 inches (5 cm)

Making Displays

Handle your fossils carefully! Some fossils are easily harmed.

Here are some more hints for creating your display.

- Make card trays to display your fossils. For each section, write a small label with the name of the fossil. Note its age and the spot where you found it.

- Keep your fossils away from dust and dirt. If they get dirty, try to clean them gently with a soft brush.

- If you cannot find out what a fossil is, take it to a local museum for help.

Record Breakers

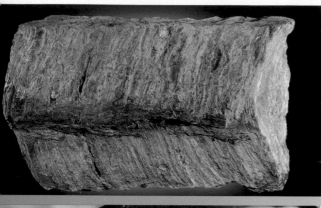

Oldest Fossil

Some of the oldest fossils are the remains of **algae**. These fossils were found in western Australia. They are about 3.5 billion years old!

Most Perfect Fossils

Animals that are fossilized in amber form the most perfect fossils. The amber preserves their whole bodies. Some mosquitoes saved in amber still contain their victims' blood!

Oldest "Living Fossil"

One of the oldest living fossils is a fish. Scientists thought the coelacanth (SEE-luh-kanth) had died out in the Cretaceous Period. But in 1938, the fish was found off the coast of South Africa.

The fossilized rain forest has many rare plant fossils.

Largest Fossilized Forest

Scientists recently found a giant fossilized rain forest in Illinois. Some tree leaves were 3 feet (0.9 m) long! The forest was buried by mud after an earthquake 300 million years ago.

Did You Know?

In some places, people build their homes out of shelly limestone. You can see hundreds of fossils in the walls!

Fossil footprints can tell us how fast dinosaurs ran. Some ran at speeds up to 40 miles (64 kilometers) per hour.

In 1993, a dinosaur fossil was found in South Dakota. The fossil includes the remains of the dinosaur's heart!

Fossilized **dung** can tell us about the diets of animals that lived long ago. Traces of food in the dung are fossilized, too.

Fossils are rare! Scientists believe that most living things from long ago died without leaving fossils.

Fossilized oysters have thick, curled shells. People used to call them "devil's toenails."

Ancient forms of the giant redwood tree grew to be 262 feet (80 m) tall. That is as high as a building with 21 floors!

In 1973, 40 fossilized eggs of the dinosaur *Maiasaura* were found in Montana. The area is now called Egg Mountain.

Some ammonite fossils are 6 feet (2 m) across. That is as wide as the average car!

Glossary

algae tiny, simple living things. Most algae are plants without roots or stems. Seaweed and some other ocean plants are algae.

amber fossilized tree resin

bivalves shellfish whose shells are made of two halves that look the same

brachiopods tiny shellfish with two-part shells, such as clams

clay sticky earth that is made up of small bits. Clay hardens when it dries.

climate the average weather in an area over time

crinoid a flower-shaped sea animal with a cup-like body and five feathery arms. Crinoids are held in place on the ocean floor.

crystals solid mineral forms with straight edges and smooth faces

dung animal droppings

eras divisions of time in Earth's history. Eras lasted tens of millions of years. Eras are broken down into periods.

fossilized turned into a fossil

fossils traces or remains of living things from long ago that are saved in rock

limestone a sedimentary rock made mainly of the mineral calcite. Limestone can contain many fossils.

minerals naturally formed materials that make up rocks. Most minerals form as crystals.

mines pits in the earth from which rocks and minerals are removed

periods divisions of time in Earth's history that are shorter than eras. Periods lasted millions of years.

resin a sticky yellow or brown material made by plants such as fir and pine trees

sedimentary rock rock that forms when small bits of other rocks build up in layers and are squeezed together

tentacles long, thin body parts of certain animals. Tentacles are used to feel, to hold things, and to move about.

Index